Anthology Journal

Write your anthology, not your chronology.
Find your prompt and write your peace.

Anthology Journal™ is designed
to inspire your journaling
through thoughtful prompts.

To tell your story, in any order, first find a
prompt that inspires you
and then fill these pages
with the anthology of you.

Write for your nonlinear life.

Published by Winding Pathway Books

WINDING PATHWAY BOOKS

ISBN (Hardback): 978-1-954374-19-5
ISBN (Trade): 978-1-954374-20-1

Book design by Wendy C. Garfinkle
Cover design by Sarah K. Drake
Photo credit: Sarah K. Drake

For more information or bulk orders, visit:
www.millennialsguides.com

Printed in the United States of America

A Note on Typeface:

This journal is set in Lucida Bright, designed by Kris Holmes in 1987. Holmes is an award-winning type designer, educator, and calligrapher. From California, she studied modern dance with Judy Massee, Alwin Nikolais, and Martha Graham. She co-founded the typeface design studio Bigelow & Holmes, Inc., best known for its Lucida font family. Lucida's name, from "lucid", was chosen for its clarity.

Chapter titles are set in Colwell, based on the original Colwell Handletter, designed by M. Elizabeth Colwell. Born in 1881 in Michigan, Colwell was of the first generation of women to be allowed to enroll in university. After graduating, she worked as a typographer, printmaker, and poet. Her font, Colwell Handletter, was first published by the American Type Founders Company in 1917.

Anthology Journal™

Find a prompt in the list below that inspires you. Prompts are organized by chapter themes. Once you have found your inspiration, flip to that page number and write your journey entry.

Dreams 169

Chapter 1
Seasons

Describe the blooms, droughts,
and all that you weather

❖ The world is in bloom, and I am energized. What sets my mind on fire?

_____

_____

_____

_____

_____

_____

_____

_____

_____

_____

_____

_____

_____

_____

_____

_____

_____

A·pri·ci·ty

*noun: the
warmth of the
sun in winter*

❖ The season has changed; this is the next great shift.

Um·bra

*noun: the
darkest part
of a shadow;
linked to a
dark night*

❖ Times when life is like dry desert earth:

_____

_____

_____

_____

_____

_____

_____

_____

_____

_____

_____

_____

_____

_____

_____

_____

_____

_____

Thun·der·plump

*noun: a heavy
fall of rain
during a
thunderstorm*

❖ I have slowed into a hibernation; If I could melt into the earth, I would.

Se·ro·ti·nal

*adjective:
pertaining to
or occurring in
late summer*

❖ Moments filled with fire and passion:

_____

_____

_____

_____

_____

_____

_____

_____

_____

_____

_____

_____

_____

_____

_____

_____

_____

Psi·thur·ism

noun: the sound of rustling leaves or wind in the trees, often associated with autumn

❖ Changing leaves…

_____

_____

_____

_____

_____

_____

_____

_____

_____

_____

_____

_____

_____

_____

_____

_____

_____

_____

Friss·on

*noun: a sudden,
passing sensation
of excitement or
chill or cold-
water shivers*

Chapter 2

Unmoored

Detail how you are most free and
where you are most wild

❖ I am lost, just floating.

Bim·ble

*verb: walk or
travel at a
leisurely pace*

❖ Where I feel anchored:

_____

_____

_____

_____

_____

_____

_____

_____

_____

_____

_____

_____

_____

_____

_____

_____

_____

_____

Af·fray

noun: an instance of fighting in a public place that disturbs the peace

❖ Wild times:

_____

_____

_____

_____

_____

_____

_____

_____

_____

_____

_____

_____

_____

_____

_____

_____

_____

_____

Re·ful·gent

*adjective:
radiant; shining
brightly with
light or warmth*

❖ I just jumped the fence and made a run for it.

Salad days

idiom: a Shakespearean expression referring to a period of carefree innocence, idealism, and pleasure associated with youth

❖ Trapped: I need to get out.

_____

_____

_____

_____

_____

_____

_____

_____

_____

_____

_____

_____

_____

_____

_____

Can·ter

noun: a smooth and easy pace, faster than a trot but slower than a gallop

❖ What have I neglected?

Tack

*noun: a
maneuver to
change direction
with the wind; a
new approach or
course of action*

❖ Time I can't get back:

_____

_____

_____

_____

_____

_____

_____

_____

_____

_____

_____

_____

_____

_____

_____

_____

_____

_____

_____

So·liv·a·gant

*noun: a solitary
wanderer;
someone who
roams alone*

❖ What has become overrun and unkempt in my
   absence?

_____

_____

_____

_____

_____

_____

_____

_____

_____

_____

_____

_____

_____

_____

_____

_____

Goss·a·mer

*noun: a fine,
filmy substance
like spiderwebs;
metaphorically
likened to netting*

❖ Move my body to move my mind; Exercise, fitness, wellness:

_____

_____

_____

_____

_____

_____

_____

_____

_____

_____

_____

_____

_____

_____

_____

_____

_____

_____

_____

_____

Ce·ler·i·ty

*noun: swiftness
of movement
or action*

❖ What webs make me feel the most trapped?

_____

_____

_____

_____

_____

_____

_____

_____

_____

_____

_____

_____

_____

_____

_____

_____

_____

_____

_____

Fil·i·gree

*noun: delicate,
intricate work
resembling a net
made of fine
wire or thread*

❖ I am living a harsh reality.

_____

_____

_____

_____

_____

_____

_____

_____

_____

_____

_____

_____

_____

_____

_____

_____

_____

Way·far·er

noun: a traveler, especially on foot, who embraces freedom and exploration

Chapter 3
Love & Losses

Memorialize the new loves,
the long loves, and the loves lost

❖ Was this meant to be? Or can I change it?

_____

_____

_____

_____

_____

_____

_____

_____

_____

_____

_____

_____

_____

_____

_____

_____

_____

Stel·li·fy

verb: to turn into a star

❖ I feel so loved.

_____

_____

_____

_____

_____

_____

_____

_____

_____

_____

_____

_____

_____

_____

_____

_____

_____

Eu·cat·as·tro·phe

noun: a happy
ending

❖ Moments to remember:

_____

_____

_____

_____

_____

_____

_____

_____

_____

_____

_____

_____

_____

_____

_____

_____

_____

Sa·lu·bri·ous

*adjective:
health-giving;
healthy*

❖ Secrets:

_____

_____

_____

_____

_____

_____

_____

_____

_____

_____

_____

_____

_____

_____

_____

_____

_____

_____

An·a·ga·pe·sis

_noun: loss of
feelings for
someone who was
formerly loved_

❖ I remember a past time I was deeply in love.

_____

_____

_____

_____

_____

_____

_____

_____

_____

_____

_____

_____

_____

_____

_____

_____

_____

Red·o·lent

*adjective:
reminiscent or
suggestive of,
like a scent*

❖ How do I nurture my relationships?

_____

_____

_____

_____

_____

_____

_____

_____

_____

_____

_____

_____

_____

_____

_____

_____

_____

Lu·fu

noun: deep affection, passion, warmth, attachment, desi̇re

❖ Categorizing how I met my friends and how I met my loves:

_____

_____

_____

_____

_____

_____

_____

_____

_____

_____

_____

_____

_____

_____

_____

_____

_____

_____

Phi·li·a

noun: a Greek word that refers to deep friendship, loyalty, sacrifice, and sharing emotions with friends

❖ I'm jealous.

Wan·hope·ly

adjective: an obsolete word that means a state of despair or despondency, or a lack of confidence in one's ability to overcome difficulties

❖ The discomfort of growth in my
   relationship...

_____

_____

_____

_____

_____

_____

_____

_____

_____

_____

_____

_____

_____

_____

_____

_____

Al·li·ance

noun: a union or association formed for mutual benefit, especially between countries or organizations; a relationship based on an affinity

❖ Discovering something new about someone
   I've known a long time:

_____

_____

_____

_____

_____

_____

_____

_____

_____

_____

_____

_____

_____

_____

_____

_____

Lamb·kin

noun: used lovingly to refer to a person who is sincerely kind

❖ Important dates I never want to forget:

_____

_____

_____

_____

_____

_____

_____

_____

_____

_____

_____

_____

_____

_____

_____

_____

_____

_____

Chron·o·scope

noun: device to observe time

Chapter 4
Sense of Place

Archive your physical world

❖ Tranquility: I feel peaceful in this place.

_____

_____

_____

_____

_____

_____

_____

_____

_____

_____

_____

_____

_____

_____

_____

_____

At·a·rax·y

*noun: a
serene
calmness*

❖ I can't find what I'm looking for.

Con·cin·ni·ty

*noun: the
skillful and
harmonious
arrangement or
fitting together*

❖ I will never come here again.

Ru·der·al

noun: a plant growing on waste ground or among refuse

❖ Unfocused: I wish I was somewhere I could think and feel.

_____

_____

_____

_____

_____

_____

_____

_____

_____

_____

_____

_____

_____

_____

_____

_____

_____

_____

_____

Ge·hen·na

noun: a place of suffering, misery or torment

❖ The things I have found to be true:

Hum·ding·er

*noun: a
remarkable or
extraordinary
person, place,
action or thing*

❖ When all five senses are invigorated:

_____

_____

_____

_____

_____

_____

_____

_____

_____

_____

_____

_____

_____

_____

_____

_____

_____

Per·am·bu·late

verb: walk or travel through or around a place or area, especially for pleasure and in a leisurely way

❖ Setting a scene…

_____

_____

_____

_____

_____

_____

_____

_____

_____

_____

_____

_____

_____

_____

_____

_____

_____

_____

_____

Se·dens

noun: a person who remains a resident of their birthplace

❖ I feel proud in this place.

_____

_____

_____

_____

_____

_____

_____

_____

_____

_____

_____

_____

_____

_____

_____

_____

_____

_____

Hur·kle-dur·kle

*verb: to lounge in
bed long after it's
time to get up*

❖ I want to remember this venue forever.

Si·ren

*noun: prolonged
sound as a signal
or warning*

❖ Building my place to live and love...

_____
_____
_____
_____
_____
_____
_____
_____
_____
_____
_____
_____
_____
_____
_____
_____
_____
_____

In·gle

_noun: a fire
burning in a
fireplace,
symbolizing the
warmth of home_

❖ Bringing piece: the collections and keepsakes that make me feel ready, safe, and prepared.

_____

_____

_____

_____

_____

_____

_____

_____

_____

_____

_____

_____

_____

_____

_____

_____

_____

_____

Sanc·tum

*noun: a private,
sacred place to
feel secure*

Chapter 5

Dreams

Collect your unconscious mind

❖ I had an unnerving dream.

_____

_____

_____

_____

_____

_____

_____

_____

_____

_____

_____

_____

_____

_____

_____

_____

_____

_____

Wool·gath·er

verb: indulge in aimless thoughts or daydreams

❖ Dreams I remember from childhood:

_____

_____

_____

_____

_____

_____

_____

_____

_____

_____

_____

_____

_____

_____

_____

_____

_____

_____

Pres·age

*noun: a warning;
an omen or
portent*

❖ A dreamy place I envision myself:

_____

_____

_____

_____

_____

_____

_____

_____

_____

_____

_____

_____

_____

_____

_____

_____

_____

_____

A clean slate

idiom: to forget about past problems; to start from the beginning

❖ A dreamy person I envision for myself:

_____

_____

_____

_____

_____

_____

_____

_____

_____

_____

_____

_____

_____

_____

_____

_____

_____

_____

Phan·tas·ma·go·ria

*noun: a dreamlike
state featuring
both real and
imagined elements*

❖ What do I daydream about?

_____

_____

_____

_____

_____

_____

_____

_____

_____

_____

_____

_____

_____

_____

_____

_____

_____

Ev·a·nes·cent

adjective:
ephemeral;
fleeting

❖ When my mind wanders, it falls to this person.

_____

_____

_____

_____

_____

_____

_____

_____

_____

_____

_____

_____

_____

_____

_____

_____

_____

*Move heaven
and earth*

*idiom: to do
everything
possible*

❖ This is a nightmare.

Noc·turne

_noun: a piece
of music
inspired by or
evocative of the
night_

❖ Waking up in a cold sweat...

Cim·me·ri·an

adjective:
extremely dark,
like a night
devoid of light

❖ When I feel laser-focused and eagle-eyed…

Un·turned

*adjective: not
flipped over or
examined
from all sides*

❖ Unconscious habits to build and to break:

For·tu·i·ty

*noun: chance
or accident or
random luck*

❖ Left unfinished; Recurring dreams:

Mid·watch

noun: a naval term for the watch during the middle of the night, representing midnight

About the Authors

Sarah K. Drake
Sarah holds degrees in education, library, and information studies. Grounded by time spent at home with her loved ones, she finds joy in the simple pleasures of cooking, reading, and growing herbs.

Cynthia Drake Morrow
Cynthia has a background in bioethics and research. She loves to analyze pop culture in the context of science, walk her dog while listening to podcasts, and go out with friends.

The sisters have a mutual affinity for good planners, delicate stationery, and beautiful journals, as well as memoirs, storytelling, and all the arts that archive life.